Contents

Plants and Seeds

Many plants give people and animals food. Most plants have **seeds**, roots, stems, leaves, flowers, and **fruits**. People do not eat all parts of all plants but they do eat the seeds, roots, stems, leaves, flowers, and fruits of different plants. People like roots, stems, leaves, and flowers. However, people eat fruits and seeds the most.

For some plants, like **pumpkins**, people eat the seeds as well as the fruit. For other plants, like plums, people eat the fruit but not the seeds. Yet for other plants, like beans, people eat only the seeds and not the fruit.

◄ These apple trees are large plants with fruit on them. The fruits have seeds inside.

How Bread Is Made

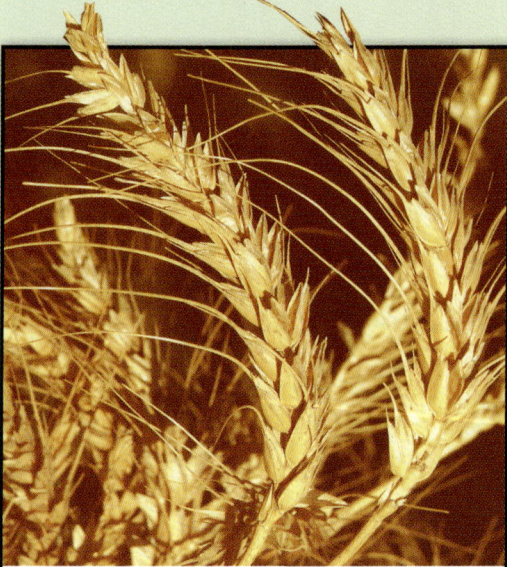

1. Seeds grow on a wheat plant.

2. The wheat seeds are crushed into flour.

3. The flour is mixed with water and other things.

4. The flour mix bakes in a pan and turns into bread.

Seeds From Grain

Some seeds that we eat are not inside fruit. These seeds are on a kind of plant called **grain**. Seeds from grain, like rice and wheat, are often used in cereal. Some people like to cook grains such as wheat for cereal.

Some people make **bread** with seeds from wheat. To make bread, wheat seeds are crushed into **flour**. Then the wheat flour is used to make bread.

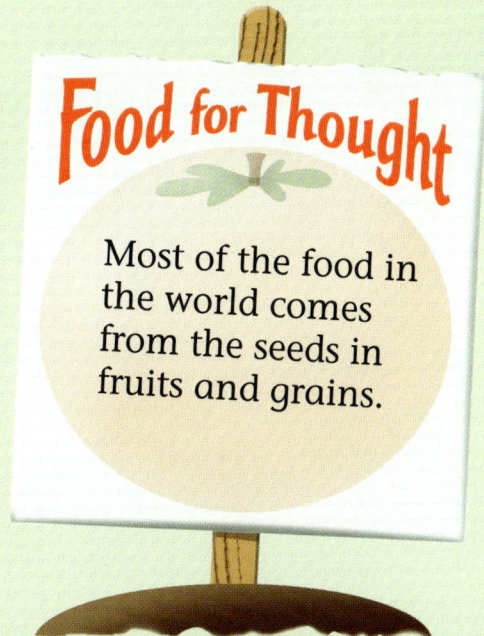

Food for Thought

Most of the food in the world comes from the seeds in fruits and grains.

Fruits With Many Seeds

Some fruits have many seeds inside them. Other fruits do not have as many seeds. For example, most **apples** have five seeds. Pumpkins may have more than 400 seeds.

The number of seeds often changes with the size of the pumpkin. A small pumpkin, like the Baby Bear, weighs 2 to 5 pounds. A large pumpkin, like the Big Moon, weighs between 50 and 100 pounds. The Big Moon may have 700 more seeds than the Baby Bear pumpkin.

These fruits have seeds. Some fruits have many seeds. ▶

▼ This tree is a walnut tree. Walnuts like the ones shown here grow on the tree.

Nuts

Nuts are a kind of seed that some people like to eat. People do not cook some nuts, like walnuts, when they eat them. Other times people put nuts, like walnuts, into foods they cook such as bread and cakes. Some flour is made from nuts. People often like walnuts or other nuts in their cereal, too.

Food for Thought

A prize pumpkin can weigh more than 1,500 pounds. Think about how many seeds you would find in it!

Planting Seeds

Seeds get planted in many ways. People plant seeds. Sometimes, seeds are dropped by animals. Some seeds are dropped from plants. New plants grow where the seeds land.

◀ This animal eats different kinds of nuts. Here it bites into a walnut.

Animals carry some seeds. For example, a deer may eat an apple. Later the seeds from the apple pass through the body of the deer. The apple seeds from the deer go into the earth. An apple tree grows where the seeds fall to the earth.

Some seeds are carried by the wind to new places. The seeds land in the earth where new plants will grow. One type of seed that the wind carries is the seed from a dandelion. The seed from a dandelion is very light. The wind can carry a dandelion seed for a few miles.

Other seeds are carried by water to new places. For example, **coconuts** may drop from a coconut tree into the water. The coconuts float until they reach land. Some coconuts have gone as far as 1,000 miles.

What a Plant Needs to Grow

Here is a plant **experiment**. For this experiment, you need four pumpkin seeds, paper, three paper cups, dirt, and water. You will see what a plant needs to grow.

Put the first pumpkin seed on paper. Then put the seed and paper in a place with lots of sunlight. Water the seed every day for a week.

Put the second pumpkin seed in a cup of dirt. Put this cup in a place where it will get lots of sunlight. Do not water this seed.

▼ Look at how this fruit grows. A boy picks a pumpkin.

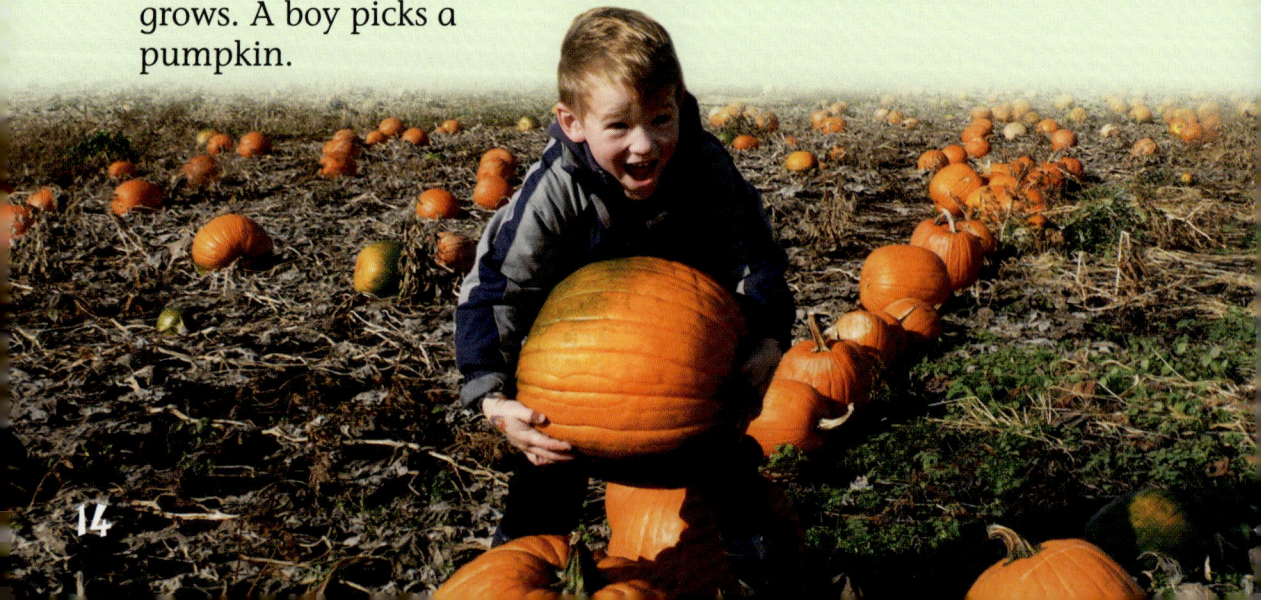

The third pumpkin seed goes in a cup of dirt. Give this seed lots of water. Put the cup in a very dark place.

The fourth pumpkin seed also goes in a cup of dirt. Give this seed lots of water. Make sure the seed gets lots of sunlight.

Check the seeds at the end of two weeks. Only the fourth pumpkin seed will be growing. The experiment shows that seeds and plants need earth, water, and sunlight to grow.

The next time you see a plant, think about how seeds get planted. Think about what a plant needs to grow. Think about how plants give you food.

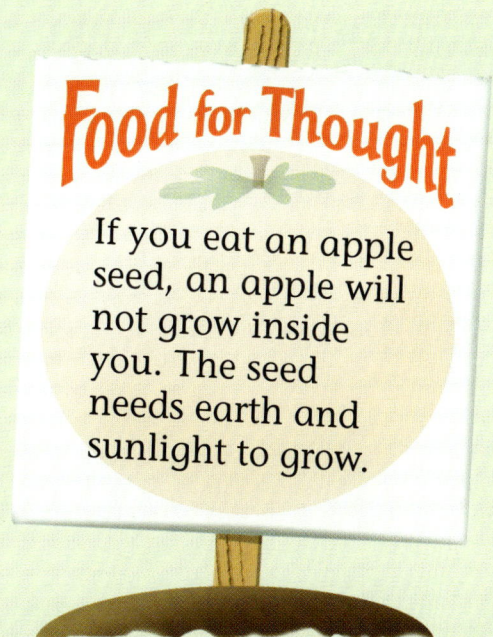

Food for Thought

If you eat an apple seed, an apple will not grow inside you. The seed needs earth and sunlight to grow.

Glossary

apples fruits with a thin peel

bread a baked food made with flour
and water

coconuts large seeds with a hard shell
and white meat inside

experiment a test to find out something

flour crushed grain seeds or nuts that are
used to bake bread

fruits sweet parts of plants that have
seeds and that you can eat

grain a kind of plant that looks like
long grass

pumpkins big fruits that grow on vines
along the earth

seeds part of plants that grow new plants